Two Voices
Circle of Love

Two Voices
Circle of Love

Serena Williamson Andrew, Ph.D.

White Knight Publications
Toronto Ontario Canada
2003

Copyright ©2003 by Serena Williamson Andrew.

All rights reserved. No part of this publication may be
reproduced or transmitted in any form or by any means,
electronic or mechanical, including photocopying, recording,
or any information storage and retrieval system,
without permission in writing from the author.

Published in 2003 by White Knight Publications,
a division of Bill Belfontaine Ltd.
Suite 103, One Benvenuto Place
Toronto Ontario Canada M4V 2L1
416-925-6458   e-mail < whitekn@istar.ca>

Ordering information
Hushion House
C/O Georgetown Terminal Warehouses
34 Armstrong Avenue, Georgetown ON, L7G 4R9
Tel: 866-485-5556   Fax: 866-485-6665
e-mail: bsisnett@gtwcanada.com

National Library of Canada Cataloguing in Publication

Williamson, Serena, 1948-
Two voices : Circle of love / Serena Williamson

Poems
ISBN 0-9730949-2-3
1. Title
PS8595.I566786   2002   C811'.6   C2002-904178-3

Cover and Text Design: Karen Petherick,
Intuitive Design International Ltd.
Cover photo: Serena Williamson Andrew
Editing : Bill Belfontaine,
Printed and Bound in Canada

Acknowledgements

I would like to acknowledge the wonderful support provided by the following people, without whom this book would not have been published.

To Karen Petherick of Intuitive Design International Ltd., for her very talented rendition of a striking cover and interior design;

To Bill Belfontaine, publisher, who saw beauty and power in this work and created the vehicle to make my dream come true — and for the honor of also selecting this work as White Knight's first poetry publication;

To Cynthia, Stefanie and Alison, my three wonderful, wise daughters, who have traveled with me through sunshine and storm, on this incredible journey of love.

I thank all most sincerely,

Serena

Introduction

Multiple, dramatic, life changes coincided. Freshly completed doctoral studies, new responsibility for cancer-battling clients, and the daily role of managing a home and raising maturing children alone after the crumbling of a long-term marriage all served to open my heart to new introspection and deeper understanding.

This volume of poetry chronicles two eras in a lifetime.

In *Two Voices*, a perplexed seeker asks tortured questions about life's journey and receives answers lovingly "Sparked" from deep within. Having just rejected her unhappy relationship, the writer looks back over her life to date, and then forward to the mysteries of the unknown future. By remaining still and paying attention to her inner voice, the woman finds the confidence and strength to move forward with renewed direction and hope.

Circle of Love, the book's second half, chronicles new steps in the woman's journey. Now the *Two Voices* from the prior pages have merged into one. The woman finds her inner stillness while strolling by the ever-present, ever-changing water. There she seeks and finds further understanding about life. She listens, learns, discovers new love — and moves to California to fulfill her dreams.

Please join with me on this poetic journey as we travel together, to be still, to listen, and to love, both who we are and whom we are near.

Serena
Ottawa, Canada

Two Voices

Speculation

Who am I?
Why am I here?

Life has meaning
It can't all be accident, chance and despair
Can it?

I inquire
And from somewhere deep within
Answers come
Lending understanding

Perhaps fantasy, perhaps universal truth
Perhaps just the meandering of a troubled soul

Perhaps!

And then I can go on
From depression and meaninglessness
To life, creativity
And joy

SERENA WILLIAMSON ANDREW

Eruption

Perhaps I am part of something bigger
Collective essence
Intuition
Knowledge
Wisdom

Then eruption!
A thousand arcs
Reaching

    To be

Sparks of consciousness

    Immortal
    Dispersed

Soaring in light years of universal sky
Beauty, wonderment, love

    Alive

New life beginning

Two Voices in the Dark

Soaring stops
Womb chosen
Confinement

Why this darkness
Enclosed and still?

Why?

> *Because, just because*
> *You don't have to know why*
> *You just have to be*

I don't know how to just be

> *That is why*

SERENA WILLIAMSON ANDREW

Birth

Such pressure, discomfort, pain
Another eruption?
Nowhere to go, confined
Can't see the sky
Know the sky, know the universe
Don't know this, don't remember

Holding back

> *Choose*
> *Let go and just be*
> *Or hold back and die*
> *Return*
> *A Spark of consciousness*
> *To continue soaring the universe*
> *A Spark unchanged*

Cannot return unchanged
Must bring something back
What? How?
Want desperately to return now!

> *Not yet, not without gifts*

What are the gifts?
How to get them?
Fast! Now! Quickly! Want to flee!

> *You will know in time*
> *Watch, listen, experience*

Become aware

Parents

Looking up into strange faces
Why these?

Why this particular mix of talents
Strengths, energy and fears?

> Parents to nurture body and soul
> In ways the mind can't see

> The soul knows
> Its journey clear

> Chooses and knows what it is choosing

> Sometimes the mind cannot understand

> It doesn't have to

SERENA WILLIAMSON ANDREW

Childhood

A child apart
Yearning for far away
Not knowing own parenthood

Children playing alien games
Speaking foreign language
Embracing unfamiliar philosophy

> *Listen to the Spark within*
> *The Spark knows*

The Spark is too different
Frightening

The Spark must be extinguished
Other ways explored
Forget the knowledge, intuition, understanding
Of a thousand lifetimes

Hold back, die to old ways, learn the new
Encase the Spark in a box until it suffocates

> *No!*
> *A soul cannot die*
> *A soul cannot forget*
>
> *Do not starve and extinguish the Spark*
> *Because of fears of those who do not know*
> *They can protect themselves*
> *They have choice*
>
> *Let the Spark glow*
> *Let it be*
> *Uniqueness is strength*

Adolescence

Struggling toward adulthood
Puzzled
Not understanding the rules of the games
Watching quietly from afar

> *Ease through the invisible wall that separates*

Desperately trying to understand
Yet needing to be . . .
Different

Apart, watching, waiting

> *Anxious to be included, wanted, loved?*

Yes, how?

> *Ease through*

Marriage

Unhappy
Not right
Knew all along yet didn't trust
Using head to placate other hearts

> *The Spark is hiding deeper and deeper*
> *Under increasing layers*
> *Of years of thought*

Can't seem to remember why I'm here

> *Stop*
> *Be still*

Mothering

Choices made in a vacuum of conformity
Lovely, beautiful children
Should be happy
Should be grateful
What's wrong?

    Head choices

The Spark seems so very far away
Buried under years of mental strife
Came here with things to do

    Turn the tide
    Peel the layers
    Return to essence

    Look carefully
    Notice a faint glimmer
    The Spark is not extinguished
    Follow its light inward

    Inside, you know

SERENA WILLIAMSON ANDREW

The Quest

Reading
Writing
Hypothesizing
Asking
Listening
Writing more

People questing
Seeking meaning
Seeking answers
Questioning without
Looking within

> What is your mission?
> Why are you here?

Asking people why they are here
To find out why I am
Helping people find out why they are here
Is why I am

I am
Is why I am

Divorce

Peeling back to find the centre
First, inexplicable joy

Then pain, such pain

Marriage so wrong
So much pain
Why such agony
Letting go of pain?

> *Where pain is expected,*
> *Pleasure is out of place*

SERENA WILLIAMSON ANDREW

Where?

Where is the Spark?

Sometimes I fear
That I am like an onion
Layer upon ever thickening layer
With nothing at the centre

> *Your Spark is here*
> *Buried under years of thought and conformity*
> *Like a young child learning to walk*
> *With practice, becoming strong*

The journey is to find the Spark?

> *Follow it, no matter what the cost*
> *Don't sell out*
> *Don't jump into someone else's dream*
> *Don't swing on someone else's vine*

My dream, my vine

My Spark

Passion

Experts tell us to find our passion
And follow it with dedication and commitment,
Commitment to our commitment

> *When you find your passion,*
> *Commitment is not a question*
> *It comes naturally*

Is passion the core at the centre, the Spark?

> *No, the Spark is at the centre by itself*
> *It came in the eruption, remember*

Then we all have one?

> *Yes*

Then what is passion?

> *Passion comes from being in tune with the Spark*
> *From listening to its melody and feeling it's harmony*
> *From choosing a life and work, a lifework that resonates*
>
> *When you stop and take time to do that*
> *No matter how long it takes*
> *You will embrace your passion and be joyful*

SERENA WILLIAMSON ANDREW

23

Happiness

Happiness comes when life is in tune with the soul?

>   *When you listen to the Spark within*
>   *When you remember your reason*
>   *For choosing this life*
>   *Then all questions fall away*
>   *Then you are magic*

I'm afraid that I will die then,
When I discover my reason for being here and do it
Perhaps I prolong my life by putting off finding the why

>   *Will the body not age*
>   *When you hold back?*
>
>   *Would you rather spend your life as an aging warrior*
>   *Or a timeless magician?*

Answers

Some people find their passion so easily
They know what they are here for
And they just do it

They seem to find their Spark so early in life
Even come from the womb knowing

Am I a failure because I am not like them?

> *Do not judge yourself by someone else's journey*
> *They have struggles you cannot see*
> *They think you have all the answers*
>
> *They're right*
> *You do*

How

Experts tell us to find our passion
So we can have riches, independence,
Happiness
Love
They don't tell us how

Some say if we dig five hundred feet in one place
We are more likely to strike it rich
Than if we dig fifty feet in ten places
Or ten feet in fifty places

> *What about Jean de Fleurette who died*
> *Digging for water in one place*
> *When there was a stream hidden*
> *Close to the surface, just ten feet to the side?*

Some say only the path of the warrior leads to success
What about magicians?

> *Some are warriors, some are not*
> *Some like to say their path is the only one*
> *Magicians know differently*

Contact

How to contact the Spark?

> *Make a commitment to discover it*
> *And to not sabotage your quest*

How do I sabotage the quest?

> *By not doing things that you know will bring you closer*
> *Step back and see, back to the question*

I am afraid

> *Of?*

Afraid of having an emotional response

> *What if you had a huge emotional response?*

I'd break through and unite with my Spark.

> *And?*

Then maybe I wouldn't like what I find.

> *If you become the Spark*
> *It will only lead to who you are*

Perhaps I'm afraid I won't like who I am

> *If you don't know who you are,*
> *Why assume you won't like yourself?*
> *Why not assume you will?*

SERENA WILLIAMSON ANDREW

Riches

I want to be rich
I don't like the feeling of not having enough

>   *What is enough?*
>
>   *Some have very little and feel rich*
>   *Some have much and feel poor*
>   *What you lack is self-knowledge, not riches*
>
>   *When you be who you are*
>   *Wealth takes care of itself*
>
>   *Being rich from within is the journey*

Love

Tell me more about finding my Spark?

> *Start with what you love*
> *If you don't love it, don't do it*

Is love my Spark?

> *Love is the vehicle to know the Spark*
> *The things that lead you to your Spark,*
> *Your mission, your passion, are clothed in love*
> *You, only you, know*
>
> *Ask no opinions*
> *Speak not*
> *Trust your own loving*
> *Trust your own knowing*

Doubt

Doubt
Resistance
Holding back, not moving forward with a full heart

> *Have you not felt resistance in your life before?*

Doubt and resistance have preceded every step taken

> *Explore the doubt, it carries a message*
> *Doubt is your Spark waving a red flag*
> *Attention! Attention!*
>
> *Look back over your life and see*
> *When you doubted and acted anyway, what happened?*

As long as I acted while doubting, I was miserable
Eventually the doubt left as did the pain

> *Sit with the doubt*
> *Do nothing until clarity comes*

What if clarity does not come?

> *Wait*

Resistance

A lifetime of resistance

Resisting being born
Resisting parents
Resisting childhood
Resisting adolescence
Resisting marriage
Resisting motherhood

Resenting being born
Resenting parents
Resenting partner
Resenting parenting
Resenting career

Constantly choosing then resenting choices
As if someone else were responsible

> *Are not the muscles tired yet?*
> *How exhausted must they become*
> *Before they realize that they can let go?*
>
> *Holding back so hard*
> *Years of choosing then resisting*
> *Choosing and resenting "them"*
> *Choosing and not being responsible for choices*
>
> *As if getting on a train, sitting backwards and*
> *Digging the heels in, trying to stop the train*
> *Why not turn around and enjoy the ride?*
>
> *Bumps and all*

SERENA WILLIAMSON ANDREW

Landing

But I am afraid to fly

> *To you, life is a frightening fire*
> *And you are a bird*
> *Desperately seeking a place to land*
> *Safely*
> *Amid the flames*

> *Is life really a fire?*

Will I be safe?

> *A bird gliding into land*
> *Stretches its feet to reach for the ground*
> *And spreads its wings to slow the fall*

> *You can too*

Fear

I hear, I see
But I am still afraid

   Of?

Imprisonment, loss of choices, loss of power

Birth	. . .	slave to incapacity
Childhood	. . .	slave to parents
Adolescence	. . .	slave to peers
Marriage	. . .	slave to spouse
Parenting	. . .	slave to children
Work	. . .	slave to company

   Following that logic

   If you eat, you are a slave to your stomach
   If you have riches, you are a slave to those riches
   If you love, you are a slave to that love

   So to avoid slavery
   You deprive yourself
   Of food, money and love

   Fear of slavery is your enslaver
   And the fear is yours
   Freedom will come when you can release yourself

I can choose to be free of fear?

   Yes, you can choose
   You have the strength to let go

SERENA WILLIAMSON ANDREW

Joy

How do I choose?

When you choose with joy

Birth	. . .	*is aliveness*
Parents	. . .	*are teachers*
Childhood	. . .	*is play*
Adolescence	. . .	*is learning to fly*
Marriage	. . .	*is infinity*
Spouse	. . .	*is the breeze that fills the sails*
Parenting	. . .	*is learning through teaching*
Work	. . .	*is fulfillment and contribution*

The Secret

I know the secret now

    Yes, you do

    The secret, child,
    Is that the one
    Who clipped your wings
    Is you

    You always had the power, the ability to fly
    It was never taken away

    No one can take your power
    Unless you agree to let it go
    They can ask, even demand
    But you can say No!

    Flight has to be chosen
    And once flight is chosen, you are free
    Free to have whatever you want
    Free to be whatever, and whoever you want to be

    Be still
    Lay down your clippers

    And fly

SERENA WILLIAMSON ANDREW

35

*Circle
of Love*

TWO VOICES, CIRCLE OF LOVE

Living by the Water

The river flows
You cannot push it
The waves roll on
Can't control them either

Life is about going with the flow
About becoming aware
About listening to the water
Watching the changes
Marveling at the adaptability
And letting it be

Life is about watching the water
Becoming the water
Harmonizing with the ebb and flow of life
Moving with the currents
Allowing the water
To guide and direct and teach
And love and support

God is here

SERENA WILLIAMSON ANDREW

Five Birds

Five birds were soaring overhead
Two pair and one alone
The couples swooped and lifted
The single one tagging along
First with one couple, then the other

Life is all right without a partner
Except on Saturday night
What is it about Saturday night alone
That makes a person feel so inadequate?

As I watched the birds swooping and lifting
The couples parted and regrouped, differently
Then I realized

There weren't two couples at all
Just five birds

A Former Love

I asked myself daily whether I had made a mistake
Whether I should have stayed with him
When I wrote a poem, prayed, meditated or worked out
Today I found a poem and asked myself again
Whether I was wrong
Then I found a gift he had given me.

   I cringed
   I knew instantly

Maybe my head wanted him,
But my soul did not
What is it about souls?
They know things
We need to become good friends with our souls
And listen

   I don't think about him daily anymore

SERENA WILLIAMSON ANDREW

A Partner

I want a partner

    Then I don't

It's so nice not to have to dress up for a man

    It's so nice to dress up for a man

It's so nice to eat alone

    It's so nice to eat with someone

It's so nice not to have to cook for anyone

    It's so nice to want to cook for someone

It's so nice

My Love

He's trying to contact me
My unknown love

I feel stirrings of hope
Deep in my heart

I wake to the words "I love you"
Filling the core of my being

I open my eyes, knowing
No one is in the room
Except the cat

Yet I am not alone

SERENA WILLIAMSON ANDREW

Winter

Sitting here in front of the fire
Cat on my lap
Dog resting on the couch
Low clouds

Gorgeous blue sky
Crisp winter day
Frost clinging to the trees
White and crystalline.

Sometimes I long to live
By the water in a warm climate

Then I would miss this

Sunset 1

I love to walk by the water at sunset
This time I thought I was too late
The sun had gone
When suddenly it showed itself
Dropping down from a bank of clouds
Fifteen more minutes until sunset

I thought I had missed you
Your brilliance emerges
And is reflected on the water

The sun has not set
It has doubled

SERENA WILLIAMSON ANDREW

Sunset 2

As the sun emerges further from the cloudbank
And closer to the horizon
Its reflection on the water brightens
'Til I can not see the page on which I write

The mirrored sun
Reaches from the far bank
To touch my feet

    A pathway
    All the light I need is here

The sunset on the river
Stays at my feet
I could walk along the sunlit path
On the water

Maybe that is what He meant to show us
The light is held out to the divine within us
To walk on water too

    Do not turn away from God's hand
    Do not turn away from God's handiwork

The world is open to us
Our path is here

    Look, see, and go boldly
    Onward

The Song Writer

Why am I attracted to you?
You write heart-wrenching lyrics about love
You love me fully and completely

    You seem to see my soul
    You know I need to write to be whole

Yet I will not let you in
I let you stay for a while
Then I find something wrong with you
And push you away again

    It is like pushing away my own soul

No! It is my own reflection that repels me, the dark side
There but for the grace of God, and my own work
Because God helps those who help themselves

Not taking care of your health
Wasting time, sleeping away the day
Writing and not doing a thing with it

    Playing small, being convinced you couldn't
    Without even trying

Change myself and see what happens
Don't call him because it's easy

    It is done

Now he is he and I am I
I see him clearly now
I see me clearly too

    How light and breezy life is

SERENA WILLIAMSON ANDREW

I Quit!

It is good being by the water
In my special place
Colder today
Drizzling rain
Windy
But my heart is free

No office
No clients
No schedule - rush, rush, rush
Except my own

I'll live on beans if I have to
But I don't care
My heart is free
And that is worth millions

A New Life

A new life is beginning
A life by the water
Could live on a sailboat
Sun just appeared
And shone on me

This winter I will spend one month in the sun
With someone special or perhaps alone
This is heaven
Right here on earth
If we choose it

A truck and a duck
Two ducks

I love my path, my seat
I am alone yet people run or walk by
Just enough contact
A new life is beginning
I feel it
I know

SERENA WILLIAMSON ANDREW

Switch

A friend, married for fifteen years
Speaking of corporate change
Compared it to divorce

Grumbled that many simply run away
Do not work things out
Twist and turn and see the problem upside down
And get through to the other side
Like divorce, he said

    Divorce, he sneered, is the easy way out
    I assured him that divorce was anything but easy

We have been raised to believe
If at first you don't succeed
Try and try and try forever

But sometimes the pain is too great
Sometimes we become exhausted and sick
From trying too hard
Sometimes we have to love and let go
And learn to face the greater pain

Of survival
Of desperate aloneness
Of quiet patience

    Until we can finally trust again
    And let love into our lives once more

Together

A person can get tired of
Dealing with people who are suffering
Why is it so difficult
For us to learn
Not to hurt one another

Birds on the wire
Busily picking at something important
Know enough not to hurt themselves or others

Sometimes it seems as if we have forgotten how to do that
A pair of birds
Working together
Face danger
Safely

SERENA WILLIAMSON ANDREW

Grandfather

The old man's wife died suddenly in the night
They'd been married for sixty years
We went to visit

Amid the occasional tear or choked word,
He's planning a trip of five thousand miles to see his nieces
They are in their fifties
With children and grandchildren of their own
He has never met them
His wife didn't like to travel

He plans to take a computer course
And learn the Internet (he always loved technical things)
Maybe even visit his grandchildren,
Some of whom are in their twenties
He's never seen where they grew up
She liked to stay home

He's eighty-six and has bad angina
Already had a bypass and the pain has returned
Something else is blocked
Otherwise he is like a man half his age.

He trots around town by bus or taxi
And plans to join the bridge club at his condo

I said, "Great! It seems as if you have a lot planned."
He said, "Well, life has not been very pleasant for a while
I didn't have much to live for."

Why?

continued

I knew him better twenty years ago
It was the same
Divorce, of course, was never an option
Not for his generation
They took care of each other

She was a doting wife and he loved her
But that day we visited, one week after her death
His adult granddaughter who was with us said,
"I have never heard him talk so much, ever."
He's coming alive again

God doesn't mean marriage to be like that
Yes we can love and cherish one another
In sickness and in health,
But no matter what
God's Spark within us must be nourished
Not suffocated to please someone else
Until it is too late

SERENA WILLIAMSON ANDREW

The Travelers

While traveling in Western Canada
Jasper, or was it Banff

Met an elderly couple visiting from England
Asked how they loved
Their Canadian tour

They said it was grand but had one deep regret
They had waited too long

Working hard until retirement
They waited to play

But now
Missing the health and robustness
Of their former years
There were things they could not do

I was glad they were here now
To teach me
They would change the course of my life
Forever
I would not wait

Love and Flowers

As flowers open when bathed in sunshine
When we are totally open
Allowing without agenda
To let the sun shine on us
Magic happens
And we flourish too

Today
One day after meeting
The man I hope to marry
I am walking along my path by the water
I do not stop, cannot stop
At my usual bench
To sit and write

I continue and realize
I am going for the first time,
Somewhere that I have never been before

It is gloriously beautiful
It is good

Moving On

There are bends ahead
As the path follows the river
Unable to see around them
I walk on

At the first bend
Under a small grove of trees
Is a new bench

I try to go on
But the new bench calls me back
I see from here
There is a new perspective

I can see for miles east and west
Shoreline and hills to the left
Tiny red and green roofed houses
To the right

I can see where I have been and where I am bound
All uniting at this moment in time
Moving me, supporting me,
On

The Grandmother

Around the next bend
Is an old woman with three young children
Sitting on a rock
Eating bananas

The children want to climb down
And explore the shore

She captures their wrists
Holds them prisoner on the rock
They argue

The children's exploration
Just ten feet from the water's edge
Amid wildflowers and rocks
And fossils and bullfrogs and fish

Is limited to standing close to grandmother
And looking

She is afraid

SERENA WILLIAMSON ANDREW

The Boy

One of the boys throws rocks into the water
The grandmother forces them back
Up the hill, onto the path

They walk toward me, arguing
The same child asks
"What kind of flower is this?"
She snorts impatiently, "I don't know!"
And hurries him on

They pass
I smile warmly and say, "Hi."
Two children smile secretly

The woman eyes me suspiciously
"Are you drawing or taking notes?" she asks
I tell her I am writing poetry
They walk on a few feet

Then turn and come back
As if called

The Boy and The Dog

The smilers approach my dog Lady
A ten-year-old Sheltie
Who never lets strangers near

She sits quietly and raises her face
Inviting their hands
I tell them they must be kind souls
To earn her trust

The rock thrower
Dressed more scruffily than the others
Has been holding back
He seems surprised, alarmed,
When I suggest their goodness
He says, "She'll probably bite me!"

Yet he approaches
Lady sits quietly as he tentatively pats
He says, "See!"
As if he is so sure that she will do what he expected
That he cannot see her love

But he sees

SERENA WILLIAMSON ANDREW

Naked

A motorboat roared by
Its lone pilot
Glorious and free
Naked

He saw me
And sat down
Fullness and openness
Here on the water
Now

Just like me
How eloquent

This Does Not Stop

I am thinking about
Whether it is a good idea to take Lady
With me on these walks
She looks so tired these days
When a woman approaches and tells me
That I should give Lady something to do while I am writing

So I tell her about the little boy who patted her
And she tells me that her granddaughter
Has a dog that looks just like Lady
And when she saw us coming from a distance
We reminded her of the child
And filled her heart with warm feelings of love

Her granddaughter lives three thousand miles away

I will continue to take Lady
On these walks

SERENA WILLIAMSON ANDREW

Sunset July 1

The sun is going down
The water is smooth as glass
A man launches his canoe
Paddling as I walk
Keeping time

The birds chatter wildly
A fish jumps
I love my river and the people here
But I could leave it in a heartbeat
To spend my evenings with you

I chance upon a shallow bank
Couples fishing
A man catches something
A clump of grass

Next couple
Music playing
A love song

My Heart Sings

My heart sings
For my love far away
A Nova Scotia love song
About sunset

The clouds are pink with silver lining
Blue sky, almost too beautiful to be real
Like those inexpensive paintings we see at flea markets
That I never believed were real before
Like us

SERENA WILLIAMSON ANDREW

The Stooped Jogger

The stooped jogger
Lives nearby
I see him running every day
Through the neighborhood and out by the water
Past trees, flowers, birds and rocks
Past sunsets and cloudbanks
And flocks of Canada Geese soaring on the wind

His back is fine for he straightens when I say hello
But as he jogs, he keeps his head down
Looking at the gravel under his feet

I wonder why

Moving

Moving next week
With little more than a suitcase and a box of books
To a warmer climate
To be with my beloved
The dream of a lifetime

Older daughters finally old enough
To be on their own
Youngest comes with me

Funny, it is not the people I will miss
It is the possessions

Never thought I was a materialist
Obviously I was
I want to touch everything that is mine

SERENA WILLIAMSON ANDREW

I Must Go

All these years of earning money
And spending it on possessions

I said I would pack everything into a paper bag
And live with him in a cardboard box on the moon
Now I want to take my sun deck

I feel like the little boy
In a book I used to read to the children
He was angry with his mom and said
He was going to run away from home
Until he realized he could not take
All of his possessions with him
Including his mom
So he decided it was too much trouble and stayed behind

I will not stay
It is time

I must go
The world is calling

The Ocean

By the ocean,
Tennessee Valley Road, Mill Valley, California
I have switched, changed my world
A woman just did a back flip on the beach
Then ran along in the surf, dragging her toes in the sand

The tide is coming in
An icy wave smacks her unsuspecting thighs
She cries out, shivering
A wide smile on her face

I have taken myself with me
I have back-flipped
Into this new world

My toes may dig in the sand
And cold waves may smack my body
And take my breath away
And the smile may sometimes fade from my face
And I am in this lovely land
And I am free

SERENA WILLIAMSON ANDREW

The Naked Sea

The man down the beach sits up
He is naked
I know why

This quiet beach by the sea
Invites me
To open myself
And expose my heart to the wind

To spread my arms
And be naked in this place

To welcome in the sea and the breeze
To welcome in life
To be

A Spiritual Place

There is a little altar
Beside me on the sand
There is a seashell and a twig
Together on a small, carefully selected pile of rocks
Someone else must have felt spiritual here too

The magnificent cliff
A giant rock with a hole in the center
Blue sky peeking through
Makes me want to paint

I am

I want to lose myself in that cliff
Lose my distinctness
My separation

SERENA WILLIAMSON ANDREW

The Rock

There is a face there
A Navajo Chief
In full headdress
And giant palm print
Lined for the fortuneteller

Perhaps I am looking at half a rock
That cracked open long ago
Crumbled into the sea
Leaving the fossil of a dinosaur

If I were an artist
I would create a masterpiece of that rock
It already is

I would merge with it
Melt into it and paint every corner
Each tiny crag and variation in color

Merged so well that
I knew it, was intimate with it
Became it

As I am now

Another Day

I love being by the ocean
The waves approach

I want to take off my shoes
Put my feet in the frigid water
And feel the spray on my face

What is it that pulls me in
That makes me want to merge

There is magnetism here
That is difficult to resist

I dip my toes into the surf
It is bone-chilling cold

A sudden wave grasps my legs

Terrified, I regain my balance
And retreat to the safety of my rock

I don't feel like merging anymore

SERENA WILLIAMSON ANDREW

Go For It

We must reach for what we want
Even the smallest thing
Or it will haunt us forever

When we go for it
We find
Whether it is right or not

And we can go on

I can love the water from a distance now
I can rest
One day I will allow life to pull me in

But not today

Stay A While

While visiting friends in Bolinas
We talked of the pull of the sea
It's urging us to merge

He starts his day by the fire
Facing away from the tide

She retreats
To their cozy back room
Far from the sea's strong draw
That muddles her mind

I dream of living in a small place by the water

Not now

I am where I need to be

Aren't we all?

SERENA WILLIAMSON ANDREW

S.W.A.